GEORGE
The Therapy Horse

George's Big Move

A New Life for George at the Therapy Horse Ranch

by Kathleen Timmermans

with Illustrations by Jan Asleson

George The Therapy Horse: George's Big Move
A New Life for George at the Therapy Horse Ranch

Written by Kathleen Timmermans

Illustrated by Jan Asleson. Website: *www.spiritwingsdesigns.com*

Cover Design by Kathleen Timmermans and Jan Asleson

Copyright 2009 George the Therapy Horse. All rights reserved

This is a work of fiction although the events are based on true facts and the author's representations of the practice of Equine Assisted Services. The events and characters described here are a combination of both actual and imaginary and are not intended to refer to specific places or living persons. The opinions expressed in this publication are solely the opinions of the author and do not represent the opinions or thoughts of any other entities involved in the printing and marketing of this work.

No part of this book may be reproduced, stored in a retrieval system, or transmitted by any means without the written permission of the author.

Published by Therapy Horse Children's Books 2014

ISBN # 978-0-9916689-0-8

For more information about George the Therapy Horse including a list of upcoming books
go to *www.therapyhorsechildrensbooks.com*

Book layout by *www.wordzworth.com*

Printed in the United States of America by Ingram Spark/Lightning Source

Dedications

This first book about George the Therapy Horse is dedicated to all the wonderful people who give their time and expertise in the practice of Equine Assisted Therapies & Learning. Also to the amazing clients who have experienced the unique, healing touch of our equine helpers.

I give praise, honor and glory to God, my Father. Your ever present love will always guide me. Your healing Spirit never fails me. Your promises lift me up!

To my children, Michelle & Eddie, I love you dearly and forever.

To my grandchildren Jon, Seth & Jestin – May you all know God's blessings.

To my family and friends – you have encouraged and lifted me up throughout this journey and my heart is full.

To all the horses in my past who brought me great joy and accomplishment.

And, of course, to my sweet George who has been in my life the longest of all my horses and who was instrumental in showing me the innate and intuitive healing power of the equine.

In Loving Memory

My Dear Sister-in-Law Annie - February 14, 2013
Your smile brightened my day - Your lifelong friendship blessed my heart.

My Beautiful Son-in-Law Ronnie - March 7, 2013
Your joy - your love - your trust in God impacted my life.

Introduction to Equine Assisted Services

Equine Assisted Services (EAS) includes, but is not limited to, Equine Assisted Psychotherapy, Equine Assisted Learning and Equine Assisted Therapy. EAS has but one purpose – to provide equine experiences to persons or groups with mental, physical, or psychological disabilities as well as persons or groups seeking learning opportunities in order to enhance the quality and productivity of their lives.

Equine Assisted Psychotherapy (EAP) incorporates activities with horses to promote emotional growth and learning. This practice can include a licensed mental health professional and an experienced horse professional working together with clients and horses. EAP is about what you experience. Participants learn about themselves and others by being a part of specifically designed activities with the horses followed up with discussions about feelings and what behaviors emerged. EAP offers a unique way to address human behavior, PTSD, substance abuse, eating disorders, depression, anxiety, relationship problems, communication and much more.

Equine Assisted Learning (EAL) is similar to EAP but where the focus is on learning or educational goals. EAL is best practiced with a two person facilitating team as in EAP. A mental health professional is not mandatory but is often the case by choice. The session focus is defined by the individual or group and their goals. Clients range from corporations to individuals looking for leadership skills, team building and personal growth.

Equine Assisted Therapy (EAT) involves Therapeutic Riding and Horsemanship and has proven to help those with physical and mental disabilities. The benefits of these activities have shown to improve balance and physical activity, strengthen & build muscle as well as overall health. Clients have also expressed improvements in self-esteem, confidence & communication skills.

As this industry grows, more equine therapy options are becoming available. However, all come from the same root – partnering with a horse to promote health & healing. I recommend you find the best fit for you and your specific needs.

This is the story of George the Therapy Horse.
George is a very special horse who helps people.
Let's see what George is doing today ...

It's early morning and George wakes up very excited. "Today's the day," he thinks to himself. He eats his breakfast of hay and oats and then waits to see what happens next.

Just then he hears a sound - footsteps coming closer to the barn. He looks out of his stall and sees Annie and Holly! Holly is Annie's Jack Russell dog and they go everywhere together.

Annie has known George since he was a young horse and has had many happy years with him. They have been to horse shows and been on trail rides and had lots of long talks together!

Now Annie has a new life planned for him. What could it be?
"Good Morning George," she says. "Today's the day - are you ready?"

George and Annie are feeling good today because George is moving to a very special horse ranch and a new life - as a therapy horse!

George will spend his days with lots of different people at the ranch, especially children. George loves children. They hug him, and talk to him, and give him treats!

Who would you like to get hugs and treats from?
What kinds of treats do you like to get?

Annie gets George ready for the trip. She brushes his coat and combs his mane and tail so he looks his very best.

When it's time to go, George jumps into the horse trailer and Holly jumps into the truck with Annie. They all set off on George's new adventure!

It's a long drive to George's new home and Annie drives carefully so that he is comfortable and safe in the horse trailer. They drive through the countryside and several small towns. Holly loves to go driving with Annie and watches everything from the window. Soon they pull into the driveway of the Circle KT Therapy Horse Ranch. George is so excited to be there and can't wait to see what is going to happen today.

Have you moved to a new place to live? What was that like?
What kinds of things do you do to show you are excited?

At the end of the driveway some friends and helpers at the ranch are waiting for George to arrive. They want to welcome him to his new home.

When George steps out of the trailer, he looks around and gives a big whinny. That's his way of saying "Hello".

What does a whinny sound like?

George's new home is a beautiful barn with a riding arena. The arena has a big white cover so all the people and horses can stay warm and dry.

There are lots of stalls in the barn and each one has a bucket for water and a feeder for hay. There's even a special place for oats.

People eat oats too. What kind of food has oats?

The stalls have wood shavings on the ground so that at the end of a busy day, George and the other horses will sleep on a soft bed.

George's new friends, Jestin and Erika, have been looking forward to having him as the new therapy horse and they want him to be happy at the ranch. They follow him into the barn to see if he likes his new home. By the look on George's face and how he is nodding his head they can see he does!

What ways can you show that you like something?

Annie leads George through the barn to the big arena where they meet Michelle and Ronnie. Michelle is the horse trainer who will be teaching George all about becoming a therapy horse. Her husband, Ronnie, helps with the horses too. They both welcome him with a pat on his neck.

"Hi George, are you ready to start your lessons?"

George knows that a therapy horse helps people but he doesn't exactly know how. He does know that he has lots of new things to learn because he's never been a therapy horse before!

What kinds of new things would be fun to learn at the ranch?

Michelle and Ronnie take George into the arena. He sees a girl riding one of the other therapy horses. "I wonder if I will be doing that," he thinks to himself. "They look like they are having fun."

Michelle tells George that the rider gets to do special activities on the horse that stretches their muscles and makes them stronger. Some of the activities also help with communication and problem solving.

What other things can riding a horse do?

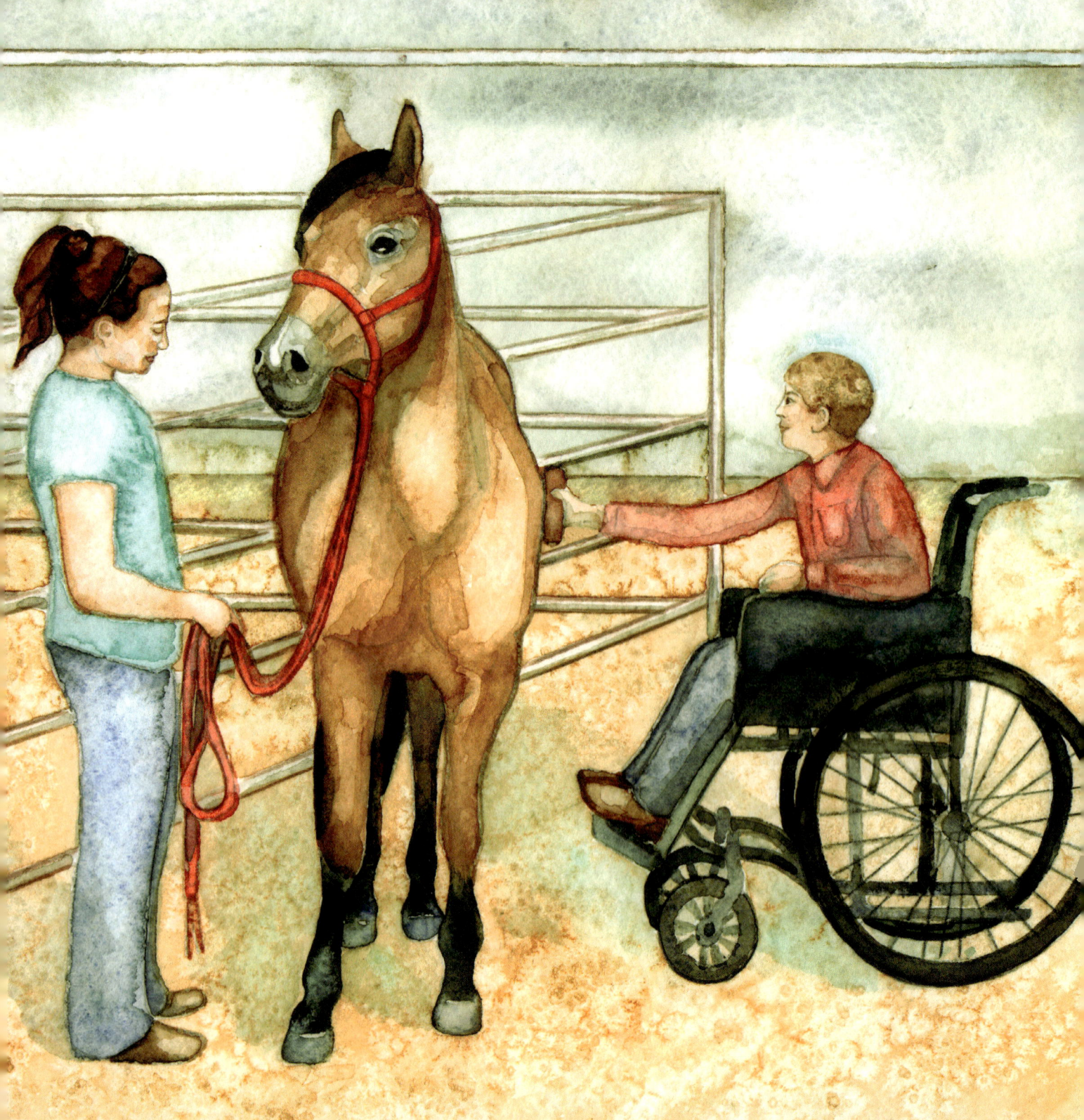

Just outside the arena one of the volunteers is showing a boy named Tony how to groom a horse from his wheelchair.

Kate is a college student and comes to the ranch every week to help out and especially likes to spend time teaching the new students. She shows Tony how to brush the horse's coat by reaching really high.

Being a helper is very important at the ranch.

What kinds of things can you do to be a helper?

In George's first lesson, Michelle explains some important things about being a therapy riding horse. "When someone is riding, your job is to stay calm and quiet," she tells him. "You cannot be loud or jumpy."

George has always been told that he is a good horse so these things will be easy for him to do.

When do you need to be calm and quiet?
When is it OK to be loud and jumpy?

In a therapy riding session George will be walking, turning, trotting, stopping and, especially, waiting patiently. "That's one of the most important things you will be doing, George," Michelle tells him.

When is it important for you to wait patiently?

A therapy riding horse helps with many different kinds of activities. Some are like fun games and some are a little tricky - like how to get around obstacles. Michelle teaches George about some of the obstacles.

She shows him how to make circles around big blue and orange barrels and then walk in and out of colored cones that are all in a row. Sometimes George will have to step over poles lying on the ground!

When George helps with these kinds of activities he has to be very careful not to step on things or knock them over!

What do you think would happen if George isn't careful?
Tell me about when you have to be careful.

George is beginning to understand some of the things he can do to help the children and adults who come to the ranch.

Suddenly George is distracted by laughing and loud voices coming from outside the arena. He looks around and sees Tony and another boy playing with a big ball. They are having a play time with Jon, who is the physical therapist at the ranch. They are throwing the ball into the air and having a great time. "Look, George," says Michelle, "When our therapy horses help people get stronger they can do lots of fun things."

What are some fun things you like to do?

After George's therapy riding lessons, it's time to learn about therapy he will be doing without a rider.

"George, I'm going to show you another way to help people," Ronnie tells him. "They might be children or they might be adults. Sometimes it's just one person and sometimes we will have a group of people."

What kinds of activities do you like to do in a group?
Can you name activities for just one person?

"When someone has a problem, or they are sad or if someone has hurt them, therapy horses can help in lots of different ways," Ronnie explains. George will also help with activities that can build confidence or patience. People can learn how to improve how they do everyday things just by doing special activities with a horse like George.

Name some everyday things that might be hard to do.

George learns that in a therapy session he will be asked to do different tasks and the people in the group will help him. George notices some strange looking things in the arena that look like toys. There are several balls, hoops and big noodles! Ronnie tells him that people use items like these in the therapy sessions. George thinks these will be fun activities!

Ronnie explains that an activity might be to put a halter on George and walk him around the arena. This can be a very special time just to be quiet and enjoy George's company.

Another activity is having a horse 'ground tie'. Ronnie asks George to stay in one place while he walks a big circle around him. George is supposed to stand still - but will he?

What's another activity that would be fun to do with George?

"George, you will be a very important part of this kind of therapy," Ronnie tells him. Doing fun and interesting activities with a therapy horse can help people learn about themselves.

Sometimes watching what the horse does makes people think about how they do things. Maybe the horse will do exactly what they expect him to do or maybe he will do something completely different! "Talking about everything that happens in the session is what makes this kind of therapy so special, George," Ronnie explains.

What could a horse do that would really surprise you?

After George's busy day of lessons, Michelle & Ronnie take him to his new stall for the night. He is tired but happy to have learned so many things.

"This has been a very good day," thinks George. "I can't wait to start helping people with the special things I've learned today."

He falls asleep that night and dreams of all the people he will meet and get to know in his new life as a therapy horse!

"Goodnight George"

Definitions

Arena	A closed in area (with a fence or inside a barn) where you can ride a horse.
Barn	A building that is used for animals or for storing hay.
Barrel	A really big container like a can.
Coat	The short hair that grows all over a horse.
Cones	Often are colored orange. Used to mark places.
Feeder	A box or special place to put the horse's hay.
Forelock	The long hair that grows on the horse's head – looks like bangs.
Halter	Placed on the horse's head to lead or tie him up.
Hay	Special grass that has been cut and dried. This is a horse's main food.
Hooves	A horse's feet.
Lead Rope	Attaches to a halter to lead or tie the horse up.
Mane	The long hair that grows on the top of a horse's neck.
Oats	Grain that is food but often used as a treat or for extra energy.
Shavings	Thin slices of wood that makes a soft bed in the stall.
Stable	A barn with stalls. One horse in each stall.
Stall	Like a small room that has high walls and a gate to keep the horse safe.
Tail	Long hair that hangs like a pony tail – you knew that didn't you?
Therapy	Helping people with a problem or assist in learning.
Trailer	To transport horses from one place to another. The horse stands up.
Trail Ride	Riding a horse out in the country. Down a road or in a pasture.
Trainer	A person who teaches a horse.
Whinny	A sound that a horse makes – it's his way of talking.

What's Next?
Don't miss George's upcoming adventures!

George, Sissy & Annie – When someone has hurt you

Sissy & George are old friends but they hadn't seen each other for a long time. When Sissy was rescued from a cruel owner and brought to the ranch, George doesn't recognize her! While Sissy is learning to trust again, she meets a little girl who is also sad.

George Meets Big Jon – When someone is being a bully

Big Jon is a retired army horse and Itzy Bitzy is the smallest horse at the ranch. Something happens and Itzy finds out what it means to have a very special friend.

George the Therapy Horse books are available through the website at *www.georgethetherapyhorse.com* as well as at select booksellers, counseling offices and equine therapy organizations. Contact Kathleen for more information.

Kathleen Timmermans
Author/Publisher

Kathleen was born in Holland, grew up in England and moved to America when she was 21. She began working with horses, which had been a dream growing up in England, and spent most of her days raising foals, training and showing American Quarter Horses. In 1991 she graduated from Kansas State University with a degree in Interior Design. In 2002 she purchased a 6 year old Bay Quarter Horse gelding who came with the name "George".

Through a variety of circumstances, in 2009 Kathleen was asked to participate at a Therapeutic Riding Center with a pilot program using horses to benefit the daily lives of a group of adults who had been diagnosed with mental illness. Following this experience, Kathleen became certified as an Equine Specialist to co-facilitate in Equine Assisted Psychotherapy & Learning sessions. It was also during this time that Kathleen began thinking of a children's book about horses that help people.

Kathleen lives in Central Kansas with her two cats, Mylo and Grace. She works full time at a local landscape nursery and enjoys spending time with George.

Jan Asleson
Illustrator

My designs are inspired by a desire to share with others the beauty that I see around me. My passion is to encourage others through my artistic mediums to not give up on their dreams, to recognize the blessings all around them and to know that there is always hope. In my life journey to know who I am I've discovered that what I've come to recognize as true art comes from the greatest artist of all, God. I believe that when we connect with each other on a heart to heart level, our lives can be changed for the good. I hope in some way that my art will touch your heart....

Working with silver, bronze and copper metals, wire, sheet and metal clays enable me a greater diversity of creativity. I make my own metal beads and clasps and embellish many pieces with natural stones. Each piece I create is individually hand done and slightly different, no two exactly alike. I also work in oil, watercolors, pastels, and acrylic, creating paintings, greeting cards, prints and commissioned portraits. I live in Southeast Kansas with my husband David, Australian Cattle dog Packer and Arabian horse Starbuck. We also enjoy our 6 grandchildren.

Check out my website at: *www.spiritwingsdesigns.com*

CPSIA information can be obtained
at www.ICGtesting.com
Printed in the USA
LVIC06n0059050814
397259LV00004B/5